For my friend, Sam, and my husband, AJ, who both taught me that it's ok to not be ok. Thanks for not leaving me to end my story.

Dear Reader,

This is for you and whatever you have overcome, are overcoming, or will overcome in the future. You are a warrior, and you are never alone!

No one has the same exact life experiences, but we all face raw and overwhelming emotions that can sometimes beat us down. For most of my life I tried to pretend like everything was fine, (and for some of the time it was). Then, I had one year where I was shattered and left feeling defenseless because of what was going on in my world. Since then, and throughout my journey, I have learned to embrace the beauty of overwhelming emotions, and to speak out about the pain and injustices that I see in the world.

I hope this book can be comforting, inspiring, and empowering for you. I pray you also speak out against the challenges and injustices in your life; that the world so quickly tries to silence. Most importantly, may you always remember that you are not defined by what you did or what happened to you. You are you, and that is always enough. Here's to breaking the silence.

Much Love,
Jessica

P.S. This story is vivid regarding suicidal thoughts and sexual assault. Please be aware of potential triggers for you and reach out to someone for support.

Acknowledgements

First and foremost, I thank God for giving me the gift
of writing and for faithfully bringing me through the
experiences that have inspired this book.

I cannot write this book without thanking my lifelong
friend Becca Vaught. She was the first to read my early works
of poetry and saw my potential before I even did. I probably
would not have kept writing, if it was not for her constant
support. In addition, I must acknowledge my amazing
husband, AJ, for encouraging me to pursue my dream of
publishing this book and for always listening to my endless
stories.

My love for writing would not exist without the care
and instruction of the many teachers along the way. From my
5th grade teacher who introduced me to poetry, to my high
school English teacher who taught me the basics of poetry
analysis, I am incredibly grateful for each one of them.

I thank Dee Yang and Destiny Roberts, who pushed me
to take the leap and create this book. Destiny even cared
enough to refer me to her sister, Angelicia Roberts, to work
with me through the editing process. I am grateful for
Angelicia's wisdom and patience as I have learned and grown
throughout the process.

Lastly, I thank YOU as the reader for picking this book
and joining my journey.

Table of Contents

Queen

From broken crowns to muddy footsteps
I've wandered this messed up world
Growing from a child who easily missteps
To a rising queen who believes in more

Silence of Youth

Silence Cannot Exist

Times were hard in the silence
Broken families created fragmented children
Stifled lives quieted innocence forever
Wounded bodies destructed the soul
For there was no saving the imprisoned

Lost in a forest of poisonous berries
Children starved for sustenance
Denied from every kind of nourishment
Left to nibble on the thorny stems of a wilted rose
Falling prey to the formerly powerless

Defined as the poor beggars of the world
They relied on the very hands that snatched their wealth
Coated in the ashes of another's past
Their footprints tracked back to the roots of despair
The path smeared with the filthy soul

Chains contorted the truth into the heaviest deceit
A lie of the mind to imprison the heart
Protection against the burden of their reality
But the shrieking of the soul wafted through the lips
Escaping the grasp of secrecy

Hush

A stifled laugh, a muffled cry
Echoes of sound, captured and destroyed
Without a breath of fresh air or a beat of independence
She's forced to cling to the choices of another
Deemed undeserving of life by untrue standards
Mother darkness pushes her down, inconvenienced by her presence
The girl would have walked a thousand miles
For every straggling soul that exists as mother darkness
But she is pushed into eternal silence with the millions

Runaway Tears

crashing voice
through my eardrums
shaking my whole body
as the tears brim
at the starting gate
as your face gets closer
blocking the light
and casting a shadow
across my frail figure
the tears begin to race
out of the vastness
and onto the smooth racetrack
trickling down my cheekbone
into my mouth
I'm struck by the bitter taste
its familiarity empowers me
seconds before
you silence me forever
I crawl out of your shadow
into the light
it blinds me for a second
almost drastically
but I catch myself
before you make me fall
and I run away
running as far away
as nothing can take me
my runaway tears
flung downward
into the dry dirt
drying quickly
in the summer sun
so as not to be traced
I'll forever be
a runaway

Silence of Women

Jutting into my Conscience

Watching you limp across the room
I want to run to you
Sweep you off your feet in a big hug
Tell you how beautiful you are inside
But you'd probably snap
I want to shove food into your mouth
As if you are a child
Looking at your bones
They jut out so awkwardly
I want to take you to the 24-hour buffet
Wait there while you eat
Follow you into the bathroom
To make sure it stays down
I want to make you normal again
You weren't even fat to begin with
But then again neither was I
And now I'm even skinnier than you
What kind of friend am I?
Calling you fat
Luring you into the same trap, I fell into
I want to go back
Erase it all
Wipe away the meal skipping
Censor out the throwing up
Wipe out my words of jealousy
So, you never would have bitten down on the hook
That is attached to the fishing pole
That holds you over the pit of starvation
I just want to do something
So I don't have to see your bones anymore
Jutting into my conscience...

Forgotten Self-Love

A culture of likes and follows,
Damaging images of little girls.
In the darkness of self-hatred wallows,
A society of overlooked pearls.

Performing for acceptance of boys,
Girls become women who give themselves,
To those who treat them like toys,
Who later let them collect dust on forgotten shelves.

Girls become women who judge their bodies;
Forcing their temples into corpses and ashes.
They starve themselves of compliments and their own glories,
Playing dress up behind those fake eyelashes.

But it's not a game, when flowers are taken,
At the price of tattoos, self, and childhood.
Our society must awaken,
Regain the meaning of womanhood.

Believe in ourselves for more than just a minute.
Come back fighting every single day.
No longer shall we remain mute.
Today's the day to leave the runway.

Guide our sisters to a world of hope,
Where we can be more than just a china doll.
Trying not to fall off the world's tightrope;
Each of us shall grow to be a stronger bearing wall.

Holding up the meaning of who we are.
Perfect in the eyes of the One,
Who holds up each of us, as a bright shining star.
Embracing our new identity has just begun.

Fire and Gasoline

My beliefs and the world, clash like fire and gasoline
Exploding inside my feeble mind
The greatest war that will ever be seen
My colorful soul will never be able to bind
When an army of crimson red confronts me
They entice me with promises of satisfaction and passion
Begging for innocence as the one-time fee
The world's claims of fashion
Steal away morals, capturing them as prisoners of war
A few of us fight to get them back
But most surrender to avoid the gore
Signing the treaty, because it is undebatable, simply a fact

Silent Too Long

I put on a dress, look in the mirror-pretty for once. I head out with my friends, and it's too early to make an entrance. So, we waste time, happy and free. The whistles start, "Hey girl! Don't you look fine!" "Where you headed baby girl?" We slam the car doors shut and lock them tight. The tires squeal. Headlights dance against the sequins of my dress- I feel completely exposed. They chase us down. We slide straight through yellow turning red. The lights disappear and there's nothing, but silence. I'm still shaking.
Maybe I shouldn't have worn the dress. I was asking for it. We all were, and yet; I'd be shunned for wearing anything else. Happy homecoming!

I'm running. My spirit soars with the rhythm. Feet hitting pavement. Sun setting. A million colors. A black SUV drives by and I turn down another street. There it is again, driving a little slower. Now I'm on high alert. I pick up the pace a bit. The rhythm drowns out my spirit– there it is again. The SUV crawls toward me and the window's down. The face of a man leers at me. I tune out the dehumanizing comments. Faster and faster- I cut down this and that street. Refusing to look back, I slam my front door shut behind me. "You ok?" my mom asks. I tell her. "This is why you shouldn't run so late." It was 7 o'clock.

The bass drowns out everything– it moves me. I feel alive.
Maybe the adrenaline; maybe the alcohol, but I'm only
slightly buzzed. I get down on the dance floor, laugh with
my friends, and sing with the music. He grabs me, and tries
to grind. I step aside. He doesn't take the hint. He grabs my
butt and I push him away. My friend steps in. He steps
around and back for more, groping all of me. I shove him
away. He staggers into the pole. He's drunk. Beyond drunk.
I'm not. Most definitely not.

He wanders away. I relax, letting the music take me away.
Nope. He's back, and he tries to grab my boob. I shove my
elbow into him. Kick him away. I've had enough! I'm not
afraid to fight. It takes him a few minutes, but he staggers
away. My blood's boiling. "Maybe you shouldn't have
drank so much." "Well, what were you wearing?"
That's what they would have said. I can hear it clearly.
Nope. I'm done with that.

"Come over and watch some Netflix?" I hear myself say
"sure." I want to say 'no,' but I'm scared to. I've been
taught to be silent. All the way through the movie, he
doesn't make a move. I begin to relax. Saying goodbye, he
attacks me with a kiss. Slobber all over my face and neck.
Hands grabbing at my body. "I should get going," I whisper
barely audible. He moves in for another long kiss. I go stiff,
unconsciously reacting. He yanks at the buttons on my
shirt. My mind is racing, but the words get caught. I've
been silent far too long.

"*I should get going*," I whisper. He continues to unbutton my shirt. "*I should get going*," I repeat (over and over again). It's not until it hits the ground, and his hands are touching my skin that I snap. I push away from him. "*I should get going.*" I repeat (firmer this time). He laughs as I pick up my shirt and button it up. I can still hear it; his laughter as if I'm the strange one. My whole body is shaking. The sound of his laughter shaking me apart. He walks me to the door with one last kiss. I oblige; whatever will get me out of there. Driving away my blood rushes angrily, "You shouldn't have been there." "You were asking for it." NO! I've been silent far too long.

Nightmare

Your face haunts my nightmares
Your laugh echoes in my dreams
That three-season porch
I can picture it clearly
Where you forced your tongue down my throat
Slobbered all over my neck
Yanked my shirt off
Grabbed at my body
Acting like it was your right
I kept saying I had to go
But you took it as an invitation
I don't know why
Can you explain that?
Didn't think so.
I can't be the only one
Trying to say no and expecting respect
But being forced to fight for it with my whole being
I'm tired of being afraid everywhere I go
Watching my back for fear of being attacked
Keeping my distance from those I don't know
And putting up walls around those I do
There are countless articles that say,
  "Don't sit in your car; without locking the doors"
  "Never walk alone; especially at night"
  "Don't take drinks from anyone; even those you know"
Titles of "Ladies Beware" and "Women Protect Yourself"
When will the weight not fall completely on me?
World let's do better.
Let's make this a human issue and not just "her" issue.
Maybe then this nightmare will end.

Silence of Trauma

Purple Tips

The phone bangs against the receiver.
Her glare is one for the record books,
such emotion hidden in flames behind her eyes.
Her stance screams anger,
but her eyes scream hurt.
As her fist collides with my nose
again, and again
the pain barely registers,
but I put my hands up in defense.
Her fist grasps my hair,
clutching my last ounce of strength.
She yanks my hair toward the ground,
causing my body to crumble, (unwillingly) with it
My whole-body fights for its life
but my mind is in another world.
Tick, tick, tick
Time seems to slow.
The other staff and I try to loosen her grip,
but she holds on, like her life depends on it.
I slide my fingers under her clenched fist,
forcefully freeing my hair.
Disoriented and a million miles away,
I come up for air.
Muffled voices surround me
like I am swimming underwater.
My body shakes uncontrollably.
Time seems to stop, and yet passes as a blur.
I cry in the bathroom,
as my body shakes.
I drive to the police station,
as my body shakes.

I file a police report,
as my body shakes.
I finally escape, for a few hours.
Now here I stand,
face to face with my inner demons.
Staring into the mirror,
I watch my fingers run between,
tips of faded purple in my brown hair.
Knots of distressed hair fall from my scalp.
Deep in my mascara smudged eyes,
I hope to make sense of what my life has become.
As the replay torments my mind,
my whole body refuses to stop shaking.
My hair is one big knot.
I can't even tell what's attached anymore.
As another chunk of my hair falls out,
I suppress the desires for:
crying,
punching the mirror,
and screaming.
The stranger in the mirror stares at me,
challenging me to understand,
but I come up empty.
I don't understand any of it:
the pain in the world,
the challenges in my life,
the presence of evil everywhere.
I don't understand any of it.
I break eye contact.
Shying away from the mirror,
I run out of the bathroom.
It's dark in the hallway, but I don't mind.

I let the darkness consume me.
Slouching against the wall,
I lower myself into a ball on the floor.
I sit there in silence.
The place was abandoned months before,
back when summer wasn't a distant memory.
I look at my phone, telling myself to call someone,
but my mind keeps telling me not to.
Do you really want them to worry?
Would they even care?
How can they help you?
The doubts are all-consuming.
My mind flashes back to the summer,
back when everyone let me down,
when I needed them most.
The pain is raw,
but I tell myself I'm trying to forgive.
So, I call my mom,
hoping somehow it would help,
but I hang up feeling just as alone as ever.
The emotional pain is stronger than the punches.
The numbness breaks in my soul.
Like a racehorse,
my mind charges past all the pain I've seen,
all the pain I've felt,
all the world has done in corrupting itself.
The notions explode into millions of pent-up tears.
I feel the anger escaping my body
as the tears storm from my body.
I long to escape this reality of life.
I should be angry with the girl like most would,
But I'm not.
I'm angry at God.

How could He let the world be so messed up?!
My mind replays all the ways I've been hurt.
It's as if every piece of my fractured world,
carefully hidden in the back of my closet,
comes crumbling down on me.
Never, have I felt so bitter.
My body's still shaking,
but this time out of anger, not fear.
I offered my whole heart to doing good,
but in return received nothing except pain.
As the cold tile floor isolates me
from any sense of warmth,
my hope sinks to a new low.
My last tear falls.
I feel empty.
With nothing left to give
And nothing left to take
I am nothing
I pick myself up off the ground,
walk outside into the chilly November air,
get into my car, and start the engine.
I let the music drown out my thoughts and feelings.
My head begins to throb
as my body can finally process pain once again.
My arm is still somewhat numb
from where she bit me two days ago.
My whole body feels like a victim of a hit-and-run.
Stopping at Walmart, I grab pain meds and water.
Downing them both, I watch the clock change.
One hour.
One hour until I must be back at work.
She'll be in bed by then,
but I'll have to face her in the morning.

I can't escape it.
I've dug my own grave, by not getting out sooner,
but I promised I'd be there for the girls.
My heart is racing once again.
I have no control over my anxiety,
lost months before from 70-hour work weeks.
I don't know how to put me first.
I always fight between myself and others,
between giving and protecting,
Slowly,
it's destroying me,
and, someday,
it may just kill me.

Silence of Mental Illness

Committed Insomniac

Insomniac
Racing mind
Thought after thought
Tied down by nothing
Words refuse to be written
Refuse to be proclaimed to anyone
So, my thoughts slash through sleep-filled nights
Hardly an insomniac, but rather a crazed individual
Stomping upon normalcy with bouts of anger
I can never be completely calm
Because my mind spins endlessly
Reeling upon misplaced emotions
That control everything
Crazed mind
Committed

Storm

A sprinkle of rain turned mad torrent
Clouds consuming the all too bright sun
Lightning strikes its death warrant
Thunder envelops the silence like a shotgun
I sit amidst the anger, chilled to the bone
My failings flash across the sky
Confronting the heavens, I no longer feel alone
And with my last breath I say goodbye
The world's memory of me shall be
Nothing but metal, energy, and an unanswered plea

Bubble Bath

The soapy bubbles drown me, but not the pain
Furiously, I scrub at my skin with the hope of cleanliness
I watch the blue darken in each cold-blooded vein
Tears trickle down each cheek, complete emptiness
Lost in my own body, I can't even claim my soul
Despite hiding in the water, I feel completely exposed
Desperately clutching the faucet's stream for damage control
I wish I could cleanse myself to remain undisclosed
But the water simply grazes my skin, barely touching the grime
I sigh, knowing it's a signal of the start of futile wartime

Inner Demons

Demons biting at my heel
I kick them off as hard as I can
But they chase me like I'll be their last meal
I look backwards, wondering where it all began
When did I lose myself in the battle?
Destroying me from the inside,
How did I get that ill?
I wish I knew exactly when my soul died
To pull out the AED for a shock
Revive myself before I fell so far
The demons seem to be working around the clock
To crush me with pain far worse than a crowbar
Alone with the demons my ears hear only lies
Worthless, mean, fat, alone, going nowhere
I put a smile on, my all too familiar disguise
And walk out in the world, my complete nightmare.

Splatter

I can keep hiding behind the mask
Plastering a fake smile on my face
Telling everyone I'm doing great
And they might believe me
But inside I know the truth
I'm hurting deep down inside
And it's only a matter of time
Until it all rushes up
And bursts out in front of me
Splattering my heart against the concrete
Into one filthy mess

Hamster Ball

Whose sick idea is this?
Spinning us all around
Inside this gigantic hamster ball
While watching us intently from above
Forcing us to keep going
And timing us by a giant ball of plasma
I want to hold it back
Duck tape the sun in place
Tie it up above the earth
So, I never have to die
I want to stop the cycle
All my pointless running
Why do I do it?
What's really keeping me going?
I want to cry out
Question my master
But there's no connection
I'm alone in this cage
While being crushed into the corner
Who really cares what happens to me?
I'll still be spinning in this hamster ball
Till I'm trampled into the plastic
Whose sick idea is this?

Burned

I'll scald my skin until it's unbearable
My daily routine to scorch my thoughts
Before they scorch my mind and heart
The water flows with soap and grim
As I attempt to rid my body
Of things water can never cleanse
For nothing purifies anxiety
Not even boiling water
And yet I change the temperature
Hotter and hotter; I beg for peace
Praying today will be better
That maybe just once
I burn my body instead of my heart

Just about Lethal

A destructive dose of poison
Injected into my bloodstream
As hormones attack me motionless
How do I manage emotions without meaning?
They attack amid piercing sun rays
It's not even close to 2 A.M.
And yet I'm crying like a waterfall
These are feelings for lonely nights
Not cloudless days with friends
But this type of poison
Infiltrates like a thief in the shadows
Though there's not a shadow in sight
The poison seeps in without warning
Just about lethal

Anxious

Anxiety is high tonight
Choke holds without a timer
I'm a goner in one foul bite
Fireworks without a fuse
Watch my life explode with a lite

Monster

How can I describe the burning sensation?
　　rising out of my chest,
　　coursing through my veins
　　building up in the back of my throat
　　teetering between rage and numbness
For a moment I feel everything, within seconds nothing.
I feel every ounce of pain in the world,
But something pops and I deflate,
Falling limp like an old, tired balloon.
I try to reform to who I was,
but there's a hole, slowly letting out the air,
With every effort I make, I continue to lose myself.
Fighting to be whole, I suffocate myself with a smile.
Inside, my stomach and throat clenches, wanting to hurl.
My heart beats a million miles a minute- completely exhausted
Both eyes flutter furiously, overwhelmed by the excess of tears.
Like the Sahara at night, they're too dry and cold for most life,
I know I'm losing. My friends, my family, they're tired of it.
Tired of my pessimism, my negativity, how I'm "acting,"
but don't they know I am too?
I want to quit. I want to stop fighting. I want happiness.
They don't see the monster though. His nails miles long
What if I gave in to him? Quit fighting.
I'd be swallowed up by the chasm of hell
I fight on. All I want is to feel.
Hanging dangerously close to other forms of pain.
A blood curling scream leaves my lips soundless,
My mind barricaded with the walls of loneliness.
　　(Breathless, hallow, and utterly devastated).
I want to cry "I Surrender" on this mental war,
but the words get caught in the fist of another.

'99 Chevy

My hands shake on the steering wheel
Driving your car—a suicide weapon
I replaced your lavender air freshener
With fast food and ocean breeze
Throwing out ten state maps
For an empty backseat
I hid you from my life
And now your memory haunts my soul.

Chains of Torment

Cold metal digs into my skin
My heart feels trapped by hundreds of pounds
Dreaming of freedom and remission of sin
I take on my personal battlegrounds
Chains of torment steal my energy
How much longer can I fight this pain?
My life may be in jeopardy
As the path behind me is full of disdain
Watch me throw these chains back
Into the face of the evil maniac.

Silence of Lost Identity

Broken Bloom

Wilting in the wind
The resemblance of a flower
That once bloomed
But drooped
Useless
Under the pulse of the world
Gasping
At the hope of catching some goodness
In the midst of the drought
So I wilt
Broken down
With only fragments of who I used to be
While the rest of me
Is swept up with the dryness of the world
And lost among every other broken soul
The stem breaks
The flower falls
Trampled into the soil
That becomes buried
Beneath another's fingernail
The beauty long forgotten

Bubble

My bubble
Ripped away from me
Leaving me as rubble
Stripped away and left to be

Vanished, my sole protection
Kept life as smooth as silk
Allowing in the flow of affection
Keeping out the sour milk

Now I stand defenseless
The filth seeping in
Leaving me a mess
The pain, the anger, the sin

Not once touching my hand
Now infiltrates my body, mind, and soul
Now I breathe the air of a foreign land.

Unavoidable

Suffocating on shreds of glass
Broken image of self
Figure like an hourglass
No longer looking like myself
I've broken down who I was
Turned myself into a hopeless being
Hovering between life and death's jaws
Always intent on fleeing
I find myself out of possibilities
Taking on a world of unwanted inevitabilities.

Mirror

I can't stop staring at the mirror
Not because I am vain
But out of fear of what I see
It is entrancing
How little of myself I recognize
I stare harder
Hoping to catch a glimpse of myself
But I feel completely disconnected
The woman in the mirror
Got trampled by the hurt of a little girl
Clinging to her to the point of suffocation
I try to find my eyes' old sparkle
But I find myself disappointed
I feel myself breaking through the mirror
Shattering the glass into a million pieces
Seeing myself breaking apart again and again
Picking up a piece of glass I dig it into my skin
Old wounds meeting my current image
I can't stop staring at the broken mirror

Band-Aids

Having forgotten who I was
My mind clutches the broken glass
With the hope of self-acceptance
Band-Aids stuck hastily on my flaws
Some would scoff at the senselessness
Constantly caught in the crevasse
Between who I was and who I wish to be
I tip-toe on, walking on quicksand
Basically unavoidable, I fight a losing battle
I pray for the day I will be free
To live in the triumphs of that Hill
For now I wander; waiting for the Promised Land

Walls of Silence

White Walls

Those dumb white walls were once hidden
Underneath meaningful thoughts and feelings
Now they lay exposed, simply a sheet of nothingness
A cover for the foundation, no longer beautiful
Maybe this way the heart will remain protected
I no longer feel at home though
The emptiness slowly drags me down
I want to punch my way through those walls
Rip out something meaningful
I begin to wonder if that is even possible anymore
What has become of this world of mine?

Hit the Wall

I'll stare at those hypnotizing walls
Until my broken pieces shatter into place
Sorry if the ringing of your calls
Simply echoes in my own hallow daze
My hands are ripping apart my heart
But my legs are running to the sun
I promise I never want to be apart
Though my demons control what's done
For you, my mouth forms a battle cry
Wiped out by the betrayal of my goodbye

Imprisoned

Imprisoned by a world
That used to be my own
But now I stand a stranger
In a land that used to be my home
I try to change myself
To be the one they want me to be
But in a land without a straight line
What can a girl do?
There is no pleasing the higher good
When it beats down
On the wishes of those that matter
Like Cinderella without her gown
I'm just a servant
Trying to make everyone happy
Without being broken

Breaking the Silence

Liars

They're liars when they say
"Things will get better"
They won't
At least not right away
It'll take a fight
Not just once or twice
But every single day
One day I'll begin to think things will turn around
But then the next I'll be falling apart
Back in the hole I just climbed out of
I get so tired
Fighting through the millions of thoughts in my brain
That break me down one at a time
And then all at once
I want to turn them all off
Before they crush me into pieces
But then there I am
Being told "things will get better"
LIARS!
I'm never getting out of this cycle
Stupid hamster wheel
Running me into exhaustion
Would it just stop?
But what purpose do I have
Other than to be controlled by my many thoughts
It's not that I don't want it to be better
I just know that it's part of who I am
Or at least part of who I've become
Because I've got skeletons in my closet
And hardness in my heart

I care more than anything about everything
Yet I cut off all emotions
Before they become bricks on my back
Building up walls around the hurt of yesterday
You'll have to break through them to become
part of today
I'll probably push you away though
Pretend I don't care
But I want help more than anything
Just please stop saying
"Things will get better!"
And listen to me
Listen to my dark thoughts
Help me get them out of my head
That way they don't build up in my throat
And choke me to death
Then, maybe then, things will get better
Until they get worse again
And if you're still there
I'll know you're not going anywhere
And then things really will be better.

Era of Depression

Too perfect for this era of depression
I'll kick you out into the streets
Maybe there you'll find something to question
What is life but a treacherous journey
You haven't lived until you suffered
You're bound to collapse in the valley
Better hope you find a buffer
That will stop you from burying yourself
Just wait till your vision of perfection shatters
What is it, but a sheet of glass?
Trust me, I'm an expert in these matters
Broken down a time or two
Watch me scoff at your positivity
A sign of childhood innocence
Soon it'll be your time of captivity
As pain and complicated emotions tie you down
So, take your perfection and judging attitude
Out to the streets and see if anyone cares
Chances are you'll find yourself in solitude
But when you get to this place of negativity, I'll be waiting

Waves

There will be days
When a swamp of tears press against your eyelids
Maybe with reason, or maybe for no reason at all
But you'll curl up in the corner
Pressing your knees to your chest
As if to hide yourself from the world
You'll want to give up, give in to the current
Allow yourself to be dragged under water and against the rocks
No longer caring if your heart gets bashed
But then you'll find hope for awhile
Although it won't last forever
Soon you'll be back crashing into the sharp edges

Quicksand

When the quicksand begs for your soul
You slowly offer yourself one limb at a time
Until you look up and swallow nothing but sand
Your whole self—submerged in anxiety
With nothing to grab
But false truths and decades of self-doubt

Refuge

May you find a refuge outside your home
A place where troubles don't greet you at your door
And yet may it not be somewhere you always roam
Feeling lost and wondering if life will give you any more
I wish I could pray away the evil and bring only good
But the most I can ask of you, is a stronger heart to overcome
Wherever the rollercoaster twists and turns your mood
I wish for some stability, but never for you to feel numb
If it wasn't for my brokenness, I would never have learned
How quickly feelings and fears occupy the mind like jail bars
As a baby cries for care, you also have always yearned
May goodness rain down from the One who owns the stars
But as you wander the earth, I pray you remember who I was
Before the world snapped every broken piece of me in its jaws.

Silence of Change

Buried Alive

As I walk this dusty road
My heart falls constantly backwards
Wishing I could find my way back
To simpler times and smile worthy moments
But I press on towards lost causes and broken dreams
I hope a door will open or at least a window
Instead the earth crumbles and I collapse
One last gasp for breath as I'm buried alive

Muddy Footprints

Every day I look behind me
See heavy footprints and damaged life
I tell myself, *Stop looking back*
But my mind clings to the weight of those moments
They chain me down, but at least I won't fall
I've made it farther than I've been before
My first steps disappear with heavy rain
Taking with them many happy memories
The heavy footprints leave a mark
Scarring my present self
I focus on foot to dirt, step by step
Traveling away from where I've been
And towards where I want to be
Keep looking forward, I tell myself
My body's weak and even more my feet
But there's beauty in tortured days
Because soon after the rain is renewal of life
And what do I want more than to have a fresh start?

Shooting Stars

My special star; wished upon long ago
Came shooting down, one dark night
Buried ten feet under; who knew it could reach so low
Instantly my future seemed so bright
It burned straight through my heart
Overwhelming me with a remembrance of a scar
Its strength upon me, left me falling apart
To realign the stars, I had to go so far
Upon my shoulders, I lifted my dream
Crushing my heart and soul, my future to redeem

Into the Stars

Falling into the stars
With the hope of catching one
Fingertips burning
As they get scorched by the heat
Reaching for a dream
Or a lingering hope
That will drag me out of the darkness
A shooting star pierces me in the heart
Sending me directly to the sun
That burns me in seconds
Into ashes of persistent pain

Kaleidoscope

I close my eyes to memories
painful and beautiful
a kaleidoscope of the past
whirling me off to a world of confusion
Sometimes I land in a place of peace
but other times I'm thrown into my worst nightmare
Overthinking has become my hobby
or perhaps an unhealthy obsession
I can't seem to cleanse myself
from mistakes of yesterday
and the uncertainty of the future
Or memories that bring nostalgia
over times I can't bring back
but wish I could, even for a minute
I'm spiraling between the good, the bad, the ugly
Falling further 'til I can't feel anything
The colors swirl by
And I lose myself in it all

Fighting the Silence

Restoration

Flames shooting down from the sky
Melting my bitterness into a pool of irrelevant self-pity
The chirping drowns out my worthless sighs
The vast, icy lake matches my idle heart
Its mockery forces me to grin
Swaying in the hammock, a kaleidoscope of color,
My world is shaken back into place
The ominous pounding of the woodpecker
Drives contentment into my soul
I look into the glowing flames, and cry,
I am home. So begins my restoration.

Roadmap of my Hand

The lines on my hand
Curving and turning across my palm
Accompanied with grains of sand
Where the nit and the grit embalm
My past into my future
The wrinkles and expanding lines
Like the roadmap in a historical brochure
My hand defines
Where I've been and where I'm going
It's because of it that I've gotten where I'm at
And because of it I'll reach a point which I've been forgoing
My whole life sits in that
Held up by that one hand to the world
But hidden between my fingers
So only I'll control when my future is unfurled
And then in that moment my empty hand lingers.

Put Together

"Wow you're younger than me
And you have it all together"
My mind starts racing, backpedaling
"No, I don't."
Skepticism fills her eyes
"No really I don't."
"You have the full-time job
Not to mention the fiancé."
My mind spirals, feeling buried
Is that what it takes?
To be considered 'having-it-together'
I don't feel together
I'm a million droplets of paint
Splattering across a clean canvas
Just to be ripped and shredded
Soaked with frustrated tears
I'm a puzzle piece
Found under the sofa
And thrown into the nearest box
To be discovered later
As NOT the missing piece
But rather unnecessary for the task
I'm the shard of glass
That breaks the skin
Of the innocent and distracted
Unforeseen and Useless by itself
Or at least that's how I see my life
One unbecoming mess
That maybe could fit a purpose

But most likely will just cause dissatisfaction
Maybe even pain
It's funny how we look at ourselves
Like a person in the morning
Who forgot their contacts
A picture appears of who we are
But clarity is missing
Because we only dare look at ourselves
From the half-asleep, natural, flawed perspective
Maybe we'll self-correct the issue
But it might take bruises and accidents
For us to realize we're only hurting ourselves
If we don't take a minute to step out of the picture,
We'll never see how far we've come
Or who we've become.

Inspire

White walls
Broken up by inspirational sayings
Chairs full of broken people
Refraining from eye contact
A loud pounding in my heart
There are no directions
To tell you how to ask for help
"How can I help you?"
I stutter, not sure how to respond
"You take drop in appointments, right?"
"Yes."
"Name Please."
"Have a seat and fill this out."
I sit there, now one of the broken people
With a lost and dull look in my eyes.
I watch as people come and go
My name is called
There's no turning back now
Sitting in the waiting room chair.
"So what brings you in today?"
Where do I even begin?
I feel like I'm shattering
From a frozen heart
Into a million pieces
Everything is crushing down on me
All at once
I answer each of his questions
Slowly pulling back the layers
Trying not to flood the room
With all my thoughts

He wants me to know the answers
But if I knew the answers
Why would I be here?
And yet here I am
Grasping at his words
As my last strand of hope
Because I've done all I could
And still feel like nothing
Broken down into a shred of a human
If I can at least breathe again
Then I'll be ok
But for now, I'll stay
Just another broken person
In a broken world

Follow

I'm trying to catch my breath
As they follow the dance of death
My walls are built up
I try to protect myself against the lineup
But the devil's slapping cuffs on every breath of life
Luring others just like Lot's wife
It's so easy to look back
Grasp the past like an insomniac
No! I grab a hold of the Truth
Drink it like the fountain of youth
Yes, I have overcome
To the man with the horns; learn I'm not his scum!
On my head I wear a crown
For I am priceless, and I'm not letting down
'Til the whole world knows I believe in people's worth
The earthquake tore apart all divides
As freedom rang out throughout the hillsides
The world tries to hold me
In this box or that one, but I remain free
God does not discriminate
'Cause this whole world he did create
As the greatest command is love
May I model the ways of Him above
I walk in peace and battle strife
As more follow the Way, the Truth, the Life
Because that's my mission here
And I refuse to live in fear
What about you?
What'cha gonna do?
When you're pressed against the wall
Left with God's call

Crush the Serpent

People going missing
Left and right
There's the serpent hissing
I think it's cause we're giving up the fight
Lowering our standards
For people doing right
You can be one of the bystanders
Avoiding seeing if others are alright
But we're all slowly cracking
And soon enough it'll all come to light
I think it's accurate to say faith is lacking
When people are luring others day and night
Where in the world is the love between him and her?
I don't know about you, but I think it is time we all unite
Take away the power of the saboteur
Get rid of his carefully placed parasite
Inside how we see ourselves and others
Bring out the Searchlight
The Light quickly smothers
The darkness of this world's plight
Cry out to the One that controls the sun and the moon
We all fall at His feet, completely contrite
For the lost may be strewn
Here and there, but His love isn't finite
Chasing us down, the distance breaks
In the unknown, comes ultimate foresight
Crushing the head of the rattlesnake

Armed Victory

And now I wake up in a cloud of darkness
Or a ray of sunshine
Either way I embrace myself for being a mess
Or as a flawless perfect design

I put on the full armor
Ready to battle any demons
Or the devil disguised as a charmer
For this battle isn't against my flesh or blood
But against the dark forces that beat me down
The truth supports me, and I stand in the lifeblood

The lies of the world can't cause me to drown
My heart is protected by the Almighty's righteousness
Protected and owned by only Him
No longer consumed by callousness

Now I'm ready to run faster than at the gym
For this gospel is a source of action
I carry my shield as a way of life
Ready to propel the evil arrows like a refraction
Wearing salvation, I'm unconquerable from any strife

Now I enter battle; the Word my weapon
As my knees hit the ground
I know God's always ready to step-in
Because he's inside me and always around

Confident, I wake up for another day
Once again, ready for the enemy to give way
Knowing that victory was mine on the Third Day

Based on Ephesians 6:10-18

www.ingramcontent.com/pod-product-compliance
Lightning Source LLC
Chambersburg PA
CBHW051225250726

48655CB00006B/2610